Apurva,

Thank you for your help &
support for Windows &
We really appreciate it!

Charlie Kindel
&
the WHS team

Mommy, Why is There a Server in the House?

Helping Your Child Understand the Stay-At-Home Server

By Tom O'Connor, Ph.D.

Illustrations by Jill Dubin

Just so you know, Tom O'Connor does not actually have a Ph.D. He is also not actually a person. And the entire premise of this book is fictional. But on the bright side, a Windows Home Server is a real product. Perhaps you'd like to buy one!

You can find out more about Windows Home Server at www.microsoft.com/windowshomeserver and at www.stayathomeserver.com

*Use of Windows Home Server's remote access features may require additional services from your broadband provider, such as access to certain "ports" that some providers may block for customers on some service plans. Contact your broadband provider if you have questions about their services or service terms.

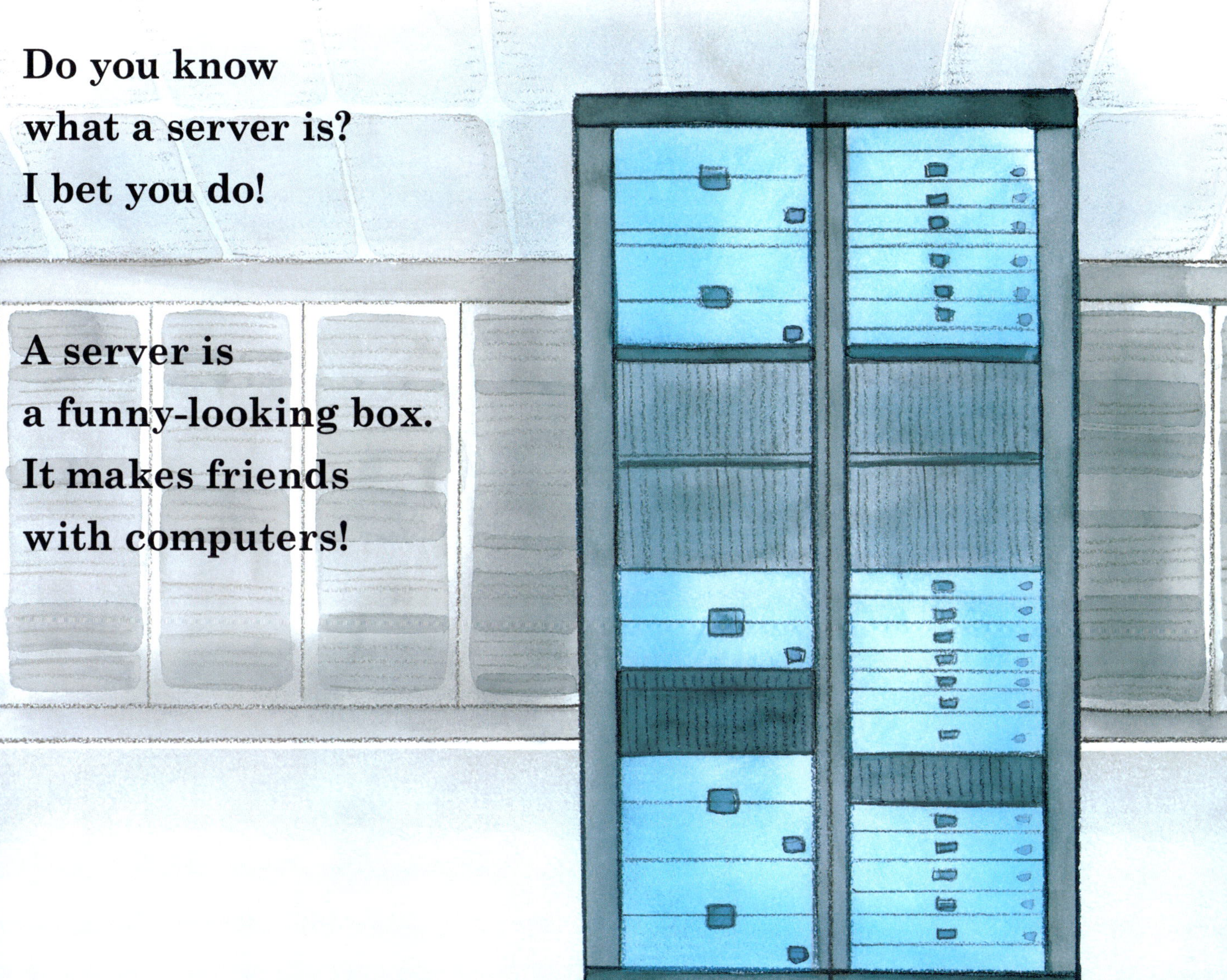

Do you know
what a server is?
I bet you do!

A server is
a funny-looking box.
It makes friends
with computers!

Big people have a server at the "office".
The office is a boring place
where big people go and do boring things.

Offices are why big people get grumpy, and say bad words.

But guess what?
Some servers aren't boring.
They don't go in offices...they go in houses!
Maybe in your house!

How does it get there?

When a mommy and a daddy love each other very much, the daddy wants to give the mommy a special gift.

So he buys a “stay-at-home” server.

Then he installs it.
It's easy!
He does it all by himself!

Now all the computers
in the house are connected.
Your family can share pictures,
and music, and almost anything else.

You can even share files
with people outside the house!
Like Grandma and Grandpa.
Or your uncle who smells like bark.
Or even...

...you!

When you're away from your house, you can still connect to the server.

And files don't get lost,
even when bad things happen to your computers.
Because they're all backed up
in a special place...on the server!

Do you think the server is great?

Of course you do!

But...

...not everyone thinks it's great.

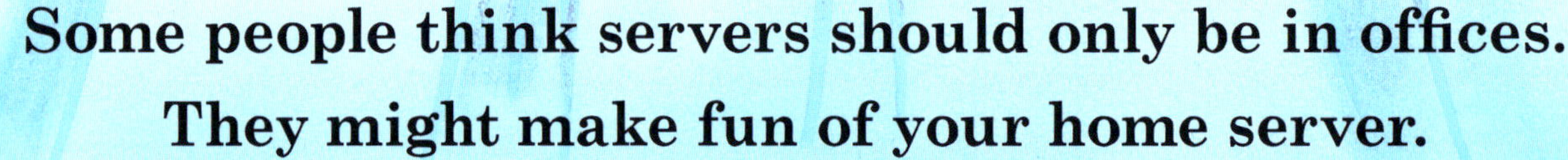

Some people think servers should only be in offices.
They might make fun of your home server.

And their kids might even make fun of *you!*
But that's okay. You know why?

Because they're just jealous!
Deep down, they wish
their daddies would buy them
a stay-at-home server, too.

They watch the lights on your server go blinkety-blink. Blinkety-blink.

But you have a Daddy and Mommy who love you!
And, a Windows Home Server! Does that make you happy?

I bet it does!